D1341895

IN TIMES OF NEED

*For all those who helped us in times of need,
especially Alice, John, John, Anne and Kate.*

In times of need
words to comfort

S U E A N D D A V I D A T K I N S O N

A LION BOOK

A Lion Book
an imprint of
Lion Hudson plc
Mayfield House, 256 Banbury Road,
Oxford OX2 7DH, England
www.lionhudson.com
ISBN 0 7459 5160 0

First edition 2004
10 9 8 7 6 5 4 3 2 1 0

Acknowledgments

Cover image: Digital Vision.
Pictures on pp. 3, 8–9, 16–17, 22–23, 30, 42 Digital Vision; 6–7
Christa Knijff/Alamy, 13 Nick Rous, 36–37 John Hatcher/Alamy.
pp. 44–45: Extract from 'God Knows', a poem by Minnie Louise
Haskins, 1908. Published privately in The Desert.
Scripture quotations marked GNB are from the Good News Bible
published by The Bible Societies/HarperCollins Publishers,
copyright © 1966, 1971, 1976, 1992 American Bible Society.
All other scripture quotations are from the Revised Standard Version
published by HarperCollins Publishers, copyright © 1989 by the
Division of Christian Education of the National Council of the
Churches of Christ in the USA, and are used by permission.
All rights reserved.

A catalogue record for this book is available
from the British Library

Typeset in 10.5/12.5 Goudy Old Style BT
Printed and bound in China

CONTENTS

INTRODUCTION

Sometimes when life seems full of trouble or pain, it can help to know that others have been there too. A word from a friend, showing us someone else understands, can help us find a way through and hang on to hope when everything around us points to despair.

   This book is a collection of sayings which have been a source of comfort to many people. Some come from the Bible, reflecting a faith in God. Some are from other sources – from people who have understood life in all its ups and downs and whose words can reach deep into our own feelings and bring a measure of healing and strength. We hope they will for you.

The Lord is my shepherd, I shall not want;
he makes me lie down in green pastures.
He leads me beside still waters;
he restores my soul.
He leads me in paths of righteousness
for his name's sake.
Even though I walk through

the valley of the shadow of death,
I fear no evil;
for thou art with me;
thy rod and thy staff, they comfort me.
Thou preparest a table before me
in the presence of my enemies;
thou anointest my head with oil, my cup overflows.
Surely goodness and mercy shall follow me
all the days of my life;
and I shall dwell in the house of the Lord for ever.
Psalm 23

7

In Times of Trouble and Pain

When trouble and pain come, there is no quick fix to finding a way through it all. We can often feel that we are going through the hardest times we have ever had to face.

God is our refuge and strength, a very present help in trouble.
PSALM 46:1

I will make Trouble Valley a door of hope.
HOSEA 2:15 (GNB)

Becoming is superior to being.
PAUL KLEE

Don't bug me! Hug me!
A CAR STICKER

It is important to be in touch with our sorrows, to recognize them, to honour them even. So often we imagine there is virtue in pretending they don't exist.
CHARLES ELLIOTT

Be still, and know that I am God.
PSALM 46:10

TROUBLE

In our times of trouble and pain we search around for help. Desperately we clutch at anything, and many people, whether they believe in a Great Creator or not, turn to prayer.

My God, why have you forsaken me?
MATTHEW 27:46

Difficulty and suffering are an inescapable part of the mystery of being alive.
ANGELA ASHWIN

Lord, hear my prayer when trouble glooms,
Let sorrow find a way,
And when the day of trouble comes,
Turn not thy face away.
JOHN CLARE, A PARAPHRASE OF PSALM 102

Peace I leave with you; my peace I give to you... Let not your hearts be troubled, neither let them be afraid.
JOHN 14:27

When you pass through the waters I will be with you; and through the rivers, they shall not overwhelm you; when you walk through fire you shall not be burned... For I am the Lord your God... your Saviour.
ISAIAH 43:2, 3

In the world you have tribulation; but be of good cheer.
I have overcome the world.
JOHN 16:33

ILLNESS

In times of illness we can feel so weak that all we can
do is wait for it to pass. It is the time to let others care
for us, but also the time to re-evaluate our lives.

When I was told I had six months, or perhaps nine, to
live, the first reaction was naturally of shock – though
I also felt liberated... My second reaction was, 'Gosh,
six months is a long time. One can do a lot in that.
How am I going to use it?' ... Preparing for eternity
means learning really to live.
BISHOP JOHN ROBINSON

A thorn was given me in the flesh... Three times
I besought the Lord about this, that it should leave me;
but he said to me, 'My grace is sufficient for you, for
my power is made perfect in weakness.'
2 CORINTHIANS 12:7–9

Trust in the Lord with all your heart... It will be healing
to your flesh and refreshment to your bones.
PROVERBS 3:5–8

ANXIETY

Anxiety can cause us to become disheartened because it can go on for so long. Too much adrenalin pumping around our body can leave us exhausted and feeling that no one understands what we are going through.

One of the worst problems about panic and anxiety is not knowing what is happening… I am convinced that understanding is one of the main keys to unlock recovery.
DR ROGER BAKER

Cast all your anxieties on God, for he cares about you.
1 PETER 5:7

Therefore I tell you, do not worry about your life… Look at the birds of the air: they do not sow or reap or store away in barns, and yet your heavenly Father feeds them. Are you not much more valuable than they? … Do not worry about tomorrow, for tomorrow will worry about itself. Each day has enough troubles of its own.
MATTHEW 6:25–34

BEREAVEMENT

Times of bereavement can be the most intense times of suffering for anyone. Some deaths are particularly difficult – the death of a child, suicide of a loved one, sudden death through an accident, or when our loved ones had to suffer. It can be hard to see where God is in it all, but maybe God holds our hands and weeps with us.

[When we are bereaved, most of us can expect to go through] six experiences – the sudden shock, the numbness, the struggle between fantasy and reality, the release of grief, the work with memories, and finally the renewal of life.

HAROLD BAUMAN

*Martha said to Jesus, 'Lord, if you had been here,
my brother would not have died.' ... Jesus said to her,
'I am the resurrection and the life; he who believes
in me, though he die, yet shall he live.'*

<small>JOHN 11:21–25</small>

*Grief is nearly always a very lonely and isolating
experience, and it seems to be even more so in the
circumstance of miscarriage or stillbirth.*

<small>HELEN ALEXANDER</small>

*Anger is one of the necessary stages in the process
of bereavement.*

<small>MYRA CHAVE-JONES</small>

Loss

Any kind of loss can send us plunging down into severe
anxiety, and this can lead to depression. The loss of a
loved one or, after a burglary, the loss of feeling safe, or
the loss of the security of a job can make us feel afraid.
Even the loss of familiarity when we move to a new
house or town can deeply affect us – however much
we wanted to make the move.

Any change is hard, and if we have had many
changes along with the loss, we need to take care of
ourselves. We need to take life gently and build in times
of rest to give our bodies the chance to recuperate.

My God will supply every need of yours according to his riches in glory in Christ Jesus.

Philippians 4:19

Come to me, all who labour and are heavy laden, and I will give you rest. Take my yoke upon you, and learn from me; for I am gentle and lowly in heart, and you will find rest for your souls.

Matthew 11:28–29

ABANDONMENT

It is normal to feel angry and tearful when we have been hurt by being abandoned. It can become our greatest fear. We need to remember that it is healthy to accept help at these times.

The fear of abandonment can underlie the whole of our experience of existence.

Dorothy Rowe

I will not leave you desolate; I will come to you.

John 14:18

As one whom his mother comforts, so I will comfort you.

Isaiah 66:13

ABUSE

Any kind of neglect or abuse – emotional, sexual, spiritual, ritual or physical – can severely affect our lives, and finding our way through it towards a sense of peace can be a traumatic journey. As with any kind of serious pain, there are no quick fixes. There is just the long struggle from being a victim to being a survivor.

I cry aloud to God, aloud to God, that he may hear me.
PSALM 77:1

The inner child is the part of us that is still connected to the longings and pain of childhood. When you… get in touch with your vulnerability and softness, feel your childhood anger, fear and grief, you are in touch with your inner child.
LAURA DAVIS

FEAR

Fears and nightmares can come from memories and thoughts buried so deeply within us that we sometimes cannot understand them. This can increase our fear.

We cannot escape from fear. We can only transform it into a companion that accompanies us on our exciting adventures.
SUSAN JEFFERS

I am afraid to tell you who I am, because, if I tell you who I am, you may not like who I am, and that is all that I have.

JOHN POWELL

There is no fear in love, but perfect love casts out fear.

1 JOHN 4:18

Feel the fear but do it anyway.

GRAFFITI ON A WALL IN LONDON

Fear not, for I am with you, be not dismayed, for I am your God; I will strengthen you, I will help you.

ISAIAH 41:10

GUILT AND SHAME

All of us can feel an overwhelming sense of guilt and shame at times in our lives when things we have done in the past come back to haunt us. If we dwell on our guilt we are likely to end up feeling ashamed and depressed.

We need to sort out our feelings of guilt and separate the false guilt from the real guilt. False guilt can come from childhood, from parents and teachers, and from our families who might want to make us the scapegoats. Real guilt comes from things we wish we had not done or said. But when we realize that everyone has these feelings and that we can be forgiven, we can be freed from this guilt. Even when humans cannot forgive us, our Creator holds out arms of welcome to everyone who accepts the free gift of forgiveness.

There is therefore now no condemnation for those who are in Christ Jesus.

ROMANS 8:1

God so loved the world that he gave his only Son, that whoever believes in him should not perish but have eternal life. For God sent the Son into the world, not to condemn the world, but that the world might be saved through him.

JOHN 3:16–17

ANGER

None of us can escape the raw emotion of anger when conflict arises – it is as natural as any other emotion. We are only doing wrong if we act out the anger and hurt someone. So there is no need to feel guilty for being angry.

Wise people learn not to dread but actually to welcome problems, because it is in this whole process of meeting and solving problems that life has its meaning.
M. SCOTT PECK

Anger within relationships is inevitable as people grow closer together and encounter the rough edges.
MYRA CHAVE-JONES

As you become more familiar with experiencing and expressing your anger, it can become a part of everyday life. When it's not so pent up, it stops being a dangerous monster and takes its place as one of many feelings.
ELLEN BASS AND LAURA DAVIS

When I see waste here, I feel angry inside. I don't approve of myself getting angry. But it's something you can't help.
MOTHER TERESA IN AN INTERVIEW IN WASHINGTON, USA, 1984

Carrying around bad feelings can be an intolerable burden. We feel pulled down, deflated, made smaller, by the weight of the burden. We have to either pretend we don't possess bad feelings, or we have to make ways of passing the burden on to something else. Usually it is on to somebody else. So we set out to play the Blame Game.

WANDA NASH

Be angry but do not sin.

EPHESIANS 4:26

STRESS

Sometimes our stresses and pressures are so great and the pace of life so fast that we can become overwhelmed. We begin to work less efficiently, and for some, that is the signal to work even harder. But our bodies are calling out to us to take time to rest and reflect, and maybe to change something in our lifestyles.

One of the first steps towards bringing your life into balance [after burnout] is to know and respect your limitations. It may come as a shock, but there are limits to what each of us can do and for how long we can do it, whether we are willing to admit it or not.

MYRON RUSH

[Jesus] said to them, 'Come away by yourselves to a lonely place, and rest a while.'

MARK 6:31

DEPRESSION AND DESPAIR

In the depths of depression it is hard to do anything. It feels as though we are in a deep dark pit and there is no one who can help us. Some of us feel unable to stop crying. Others feel that if only tears would come they might be some kind of release. Our sleep can be disturbed, our eating habits might change and things that used to appeal to us now seem totally uninteresting. People tell us to pull ourselves together – and we wish it were that easy. We feel worthless, guilty, ashamed and utterly isolated, and it is crucial to get medical help.

Like any pain, depression is saying something to us and we need to listen to our bodies. Is it telling us to change our lifestyles or relationships? Do we need to work on our self-esteem?

Why are you cast down, O my soul,
and why are you disquieted within me?
Hope in God; for I shall again praise him,
my help and my God.
PSALM 42:5–6

The Lord will give beauty for ashes, joy instead of mourning, a garment of praise instead of a spirit of despair.
ISAIAH 61:3

The wounds of the heart are part of the reality of life and cannot be prevented.
JEAN VANIER

SELF-ESTEEM

Our self-esteem may be low
because of things in our past –
maybe traumatic things that still
give us pain. But we can gradually
transform our lives by being kind
to ourselves, learning to see that
we do not need to be perfect –
being 'good enough' is all we need
to be.

God made us, knows us,
and loves each of us as unique
children, made in love.

*I cannot think of a way of being in
life that is more destructive to our
self-respect and the general quality
of our life than seeing ourselves as
victims.*
SUSAN JEFFERS

*When I was being made in secret in
my mother's womb you knew all about me,
Lord God.*
PSALM 139:15

What I am is good enough if I would only be it openly.
CARL ROGERS

*If God is my rock, my refuge and my strength, then
I have no need to be defensive, for I know that he
accepts me as I am and that I am precious in his eyes,
that his power is greatest in my weakness and it is
through my weakness that I come to a knowledge of
my true identity and worth.*

GERARD HUGHES

CONFUSION AND TEMPTATION

It is hard to make decisions when we are confused, and we are sometimes tempted to do something we might regret later.

We have not a high priest who is unable to sympathize with our weaknesses, but one who in every respect has been tempted as we are, yet without sin. Let us then with confidence draw near to the throne of grace, that we may receive mercy and find grace to help in time of need.
HEBREWS 4:15, 16

Be strong and of good courage; be not frightened, neither be dismayed; for the Lord your God is with you wherever you go.
JOSHUA 1:9

God is faithful, and he will not let you be tempted beyond your strength, but with the temptation will also provide the way of escape, that you may be able to endure it.
1 CORINTHIANS 10:13

CRITICISM

Criticism can be so painful. We feel hurt and rejected. It might be that our self-esteem is low and that we hear every criticism as a condemnation of ourselves as persons. If we feel condemned for who we are, this can be one of the most painful of all emotions.

You must understand *what is happening to you before you can feel it… If your perception is twisted and distorted in some way, your emotional reaction will be abnormal.*

<small>DAVID D. BURNS</small>

Cast your burden on the Lord, and he will sustain you.

<small>PSALM 55:22</small>

If God is for us, who is against us?

<small>ROMANS 8:31</small>

BITTERNESS

It can be all too easy to hold onto old hatred and bitterness. When we are hurt in some way, it is natural to feel angry and resentful. If the hurt changes the course of our lives dramatically, it is hard to 'let go'. But we must do this in order to stop the natural rage changing in time into bitterness.

Bitterness can trap us into negative thinking that will go on doing more and more damage to our inner lives. Somehow we have to 'let go' if we are to come out of it and be set free. This 'letting go' doesn't happen in an instant – it can take months and years.

When my soul was embittered,
when I was pricked in heart,
I was stupid and ignorant,

I was like a beast towards thee.
Nevertheless I am continually with thee;
thou dost hold my right hand.
Thou dost guide me with thy counsel,
and afterward thou wilt receive me to glory.
Psalm 73:21–24

See to it that no 'roots of bitterness' spring up and cause
trouble.
Hebrews 12:15

WEAKNESS

It is easy sometimes to interpret a significant failure as
an earth-shattering disaster. Our weakness can make us
hate ourselves and fear that we may never recover. But
we can adapt, we can decide to change – to get beyond
failure and move on in our lives.

The main thing in life is not to be afraid to be human.
Pablo Casals

All we like sheep have gone astray; we have turned
every one to his own way; and the Lord has laid on him
the iniquity of us all.
Isaiah 53:6

A sense of inadequacy is well-nigh universal.
Henry McKeating

Be our strength in hours of weakness,
In our wanderings be our guide;
Through endeavour, failure, danger,
Father, be thou at our side.
LOVE M. WILLIS

Our greatest weakness lies in giving up. The most certain
way to succeed is always to try just one more time.
THOMAS EDISON

LONELINESS

Loneliness can be one of the worst feelings to have to
face long term. Maybe we have faced death or desertion,
maybe we want a partner, or feel rejected, unwanted –
as if we do not deserve to have friends. The constant
loneliness can lead to anxiety and depression.

We… cannot expect the world to flock to our door;
the first steps must be ours.
JOAN GIBSON

Draw near to God and he will draw near to you.
JAMES 4:8

I wait for the Lord, my soul waits, and in his word
I hope; my soul waits for the Lord more than watchmen
for the morning.
PSALM 130:5–6

DOUBT

When we are full of doubt, or in trouble or pain, we sometimes see the world in sharp focus – pains seem greater, irritations seem more significant, and all this is happening at a time when we crave some comfort.

The important thing is not to stop questioning.
ALBERT EINSTEIN

If you would be a real seeker after truth, it is necessary that at least once in your life you doubt, as far as possible, all things.
RENE DESCARTES

Put your finger here, and see my hands; and put out your hand, and place it in my side; do not be faithless, but believing… Blessed are those who have not seen and yet believe.
JOHN 20:27–29

The testing of your faith produces steadfastness.
JAMES 1:3

FINDING A WAY THROUGH

When we go through times of trouble, we often ask ourselves why we have to suffer in this way. We wonder what it is that God wants of us. It is hard to understand why the God who is Love can allow pain and suffering.

The answer is in the pain.
GERARD HUGHES

Where is God when it hurts? … He transforms pain, using it to teach and strengthen us, if we allow it to turn us towards him.
PHILIP YANCEY

PAIN THAT HEALS

There is some comfort for us in the idea of 'the wounded healer'. If we have suffered trouble and pain, we can more easily relate to others who are suffering. And through our woundedness, other people can see that our vulnerability can be an asset – not something to hide.

Suffering concentrates our attention on the one thing necessary for healing: the Spirit of God who alone can deliver us from the body of corruption to the place of freedom. The transition may be painful, but the destination is beyond all description in its splendour and completeness.
MARTIN ISRAEL

The extreme greatness of Christianity lies in the fact that it does not seek a supernatural remedy for suffering but a supernatural use for it.

SIMONE WEIL

Let suffering be a teacher.

IVAN MANN

STRENGTH

Struggling through times of difficulty in our lives, or trying to help someone who is suffering or who needs long-term care, can be hugely demanding. Sometimes we can feel useless, or that we always get it wrong, and we can become exhausted and drained.

They who wait for the Lord shall renew their strength,
they shall mount up with wings like eagles,
they shall run and not be weary,
they shall walk and not faint.

ISAIAH 40:31

The joy of the Lord is your strength.

NEHEMIAH 8:10

God is my salvation; I will trust, and will not be afraid;
for the Lord God is my strength and my song, and he has
become my salvation.

ISAIAH 12:2

GUIDANCE

When we are unsure about big decisions, it is usually best to talk through the options with at least one other person. Advice to 'sleep on it' is sound, because as we turn things over in our minds, we see things more clearly.

I will instruct you and teach you the way you should go;
I will counsel you with my eye upon you.
Be not like a horse or a mule without understanding.
PSALM 32:8–9

God rarely shows us the way with a loud shout or a
bright light. Rather, he comes almost unnoticed like
a whisper, a promise of hope.
DOUG SEWELL

Be thou our guardian and our guide,
And hear us when we call;
Let not our slippery footsteps slide,
And hold us lest we fall.
I. WILLIAMS

LIFE

Sometimes when we are working our way through difficult times, and we dare to share our vulnerability with others, we can find that the act of sharing is itself the healing thing.

I am the bread of life; he who comes to me shall not hunger, and he who believes in me shall never thirst.
JOHN 6:35

Since I have had cancer, I take each day as it comes. When I wake up, I am so glad I have another day. I make the most of every moment, and I know it will sound odd, but I am happy. I make sure I see plenty of the family as often as I can, and even little things, like seeing the flowers in the garden, give me a great sense of being so alive and glad for every extra day that God gives me.
A WOMAN ON A TELEVISION PROGRAMME

I have come to give you abundant life.
JOHN 10:10

Hope [is] a belief that there is purpose in all life, that good will prevail over evil, and that life is a journey that is leading us home.
JOAN GIBSON

FRIENDSHIP

A friend can bring us and others so much joy that it is worth deliberately cultivating friendships. We will find that there are many other lonely people in the world.

Friendship is a miracle.
SIMONE WEIL

Two are better than one… if you fall down your friend can help you up.

ECCLESIASTES 4:9–10

Greater love has no man than this, that a man lay down his life for his friends. You are my friends… for all that I have heard from my Father I have made known to you.

JOHN 15:13–15

A friend may well be reckoned the masterpiece of Nature.

RALPH WALDO EMERSON

PRAYER

Prayer need not be about words. It can be just being in God's presence, looking at a flower or a butterfly, or enjoying the evening sun, or a painting, or the smile of a child. Our innermost thoughts are known to God, and when we seek to grow spiritually, our Creator hears us and smiles at us.

When you sink yourself into silent prayer, all of what you are is lit by the fire of God's love. In that light you will be able to see just what it is that you need and just what it is that you do not need.

MELVYN MATTHEWS

Have no anxiety about anything, but in everything by prayer and supplication with thanksgiving let your requests be made known to God.
PHILIPPIANS 4:6

Ask and you will receive, so that your happiness may be complete.
JOHN 16:24 (GNB)

When you pray, go into your room and shut the door and pray to your Father who is in secret; and your Father who sees in secret will reward you.
MATTHEW 6:6

Jesus went up into the hills by himself to pray on his own.
MATTHEW 14:23

FAITH

Some of us find faith difficult, thinking that it is something other people have, not realizing that we have it too. Faith is something that grows inside us imperceptibly. The very thought that we don't have what other people have is a sign of our faith starting to grow.

Faith is the assurance of things hoped for, the conviction of things not seen.
HEBREWS 11:1

THANKSGIVING

Setting out to be thankful for our lives and for the loveliness in the world can help to lift our spirits. Even when we are in such difficult situations that despair is easier, deliberately trying to be thankful for simple things, such as a sparrow on the window sill, can transform our outlook.

There are nettles everywhere
But smooth, green grasses are more common still
The blue of heaven is larger than the cloud.
ELIZABETH BARRETT BROWNING

Love of God is pure when joy and suffering inspire
an equal degree of gratitude.
SIMONE WEIL

RECONCILIATION

A determination not to find reconciliation can lead to crippling bitterness. A willingness to try to find a way forward can be healing – and someone has to make the first step.

In Christ God was reconciling the world to himself, not
counting their trespasses against them, and entrusting
to us the message of reconciliation.
2 CORINTHIANS 5:19

Leave your gift there before the altar and go; first be reconciled to your brother, and then come and offer your gift.

MATTHEW 5:24

When I survey the wondrous cross
On which the Prince of glory died
My richest gain I count but loss
And pour contempt on all my pride.

ISAAC WATTS

FORGIVENESS

Forgiving someone who has hurt us deeply can be one of the hardest things to do. But rushing or being pushed into forgiving can be counterproductive. Both parties need to accept the depth of the hurt.

It can be that our *intention* to forgive is all we can manage for now. We know we are wanting to 'let go' – and we are working on it.

Forgiveness is healing.

RUSS PARKER

Take your life in your own hands, and what happens? A terrible thing: no one to blame.

ERICA JONG

Vengeance is too little. Pardon is very much bigger and greater.

MADAME IRENE LAURE

Peter came to Jesus and asked him, 'Lord, if someone does me wrong, how many times do I forgive him? Seven times?' Jesus said to him, 'Not seven times, but seventy times seven.'

MATTHEW 18:21–22

Forgiveness is not an occasional act; it is a permanent attitude.

MARTIN LUTHER KING

He who cannot forgive another breaks the bridge over which he must pass himself.

GEORGE HERBERT

Father, forgive them, because they don't know what they are doing.

LUKE 23:34

Hoping in God

Whatever we do, we must cling on to hope. Of course, at times we will despair, but if we can turn that around and hope, that will bring healing.

May the God of hope fill you with all joy and peace in believing, so that by the power of the Holy Spirit you may abound in hope.

Romans 15:13

The eternal God is your dwelling place, and underneath are the everlasting arms.

Deuteronomy 33:27

None other Lamb, none other Name,
None other Hope in heaven or earth or sea,
None other hiding place from sin and shame,
None beside thee.

Christina Rossetti

Grace

Grace is God's free gift to all of us – God loves us and cherishes us, forgives and protects us, and holds onto us as we struggle with guilt and confusion.

Who shall separate us from the love of Christ? Shall tribulation, or distress, or persecution, or famine, or nakedness, or peril, or sword?

ROMANS 8:35

Guilt is universal… repressed, it leads to anger, rebellion, fear and anxiety, a deadening of conscience, an increasing inability to recognize one's faults, and a growing dominance of aggressive tendencies. [But if we consciously recognize our guilt, that] leads to repentance, to the peace and security of divine pardon, and in that way to a progressive refinement of conscience and a steady weakening of aggressive impulses. [So] the enemy guilt becomes a friend because it leads to an experience of grace.

PAUL TOURNIER

You know the grace of our Lord Jesus Christ, that though he was rich, yet for your sake he became poor, so that by his poverty you might become rich.

2 CORINTHIANS 8:9

PEACE

Negotiation and reconciliation to reach a position of peace can be a struggle. But finding a place of peace can be blissful.

Please choose the way of peace.

MOTHER TERESA IN A LETTER TO GEORGE BUSH AND SADDAM HUSSEIN, JANUARY 1991

Peace be with you.
JOHN 20:19

The peace of God, which passes all understanding,
will keep your hearts and minds in Christ Jesus.
PHILIPPIANS 4:7

Drop thy still dews of quietness,
Till all our strivings cease;
Take from our souls the strain and stress,
And let our ordered lives confess
The beauty of thy peace.
JOHN GREENLEAF WHITTIER

Consolation

As we hope for a better future, any kind of consolation can be a gift – a reassurance that others around us join us in our hope.

But all shall be well, and all shall be well and all manner of things shall be well.
DAME JULIAN OF NORWICH

I have loved you with an everlasting love.
JEREMIAH 31:3

God gave us eternal life, and this life is in his Son.
1 JOHN 5:11

Love

Love goes on and on down the generations, passed on from person to person, giving strength to go on with life, even when it is tough. Love is the greatest gift we can give to another person.

God loves us with a pure love that has no wish to dominate, manipulate or coerce us into a loving relationship with him. He loves, he waits and leaves us to respond when we are ready. But he goes on loving, whatever our response.
GRACE SHEPPARD

This is my commandment, that you love one another as I have loved you.

JOHN 15:12

This is what love is: it is not that we have loved God, but that he loved us and sent his Son to be the means by which our sins are forgiven.

1 JOHN 4:10 (GNB)

The truth is that our well-being is dependent on our giving love. It is not about what comes back; it is about what goes out.

ALAN COHEN

It makes a vast difference whether we suppose that God loves us because we are lovable, or that he loves, in spite of much in us which deserves his antagonism, because he is overflowing love.

WILLIAM TEMPLE

TRUST

Learning to trust after we have been hurt can be hard. For those abused in childhood, trusting anyone can feel impossible. But when there seems no way forward, if we can put our hand into the hand of God, we will grow and change and learn to trust.

I said to the man who stood at the Gate of the Year, 'Give me a light that I may tread safely into the unknown.'

And he replied, 'Go out into the darkness,
and put your hand into the hand of God.
That shall be to you better than light,
and safer than a known way.'

MINNIE LOUISE HASKINS, READ BY KING GEORGE VI IN HIS
CHRISTMAS BROADCAST OF 1939

Trust in the Lord for ever, for the Lord God is an
everlasting rock.

ISAIAH 26:4

He who did not spare his own Son but gave him up for
us all, will he not also give us all things with him?

ROMANS 8:32

This is God, our God for ever and ever. He will be our
guide for ever.

PSALM 48:14

JOY

Even the tiniest sense of joy can lift us from despair
towards hope, and from depression towards a place
of peace.

I have told you this so that my joy may be in you and
that your joy may be complete.

JOHN 15:11

You never enjoy the world aright, till the Sea itself floweth in your veins, till you are clothed with the heavens, and crowned with the stars; and perceive yourself to be the sole heir of the whole world, and more than so, because men are in it who are every one sole heirs as well as you. Till you can sing and rejoice and delight in God, as misers do in gold, and Kings in sceptres, you never enjoy the world.

THOMAS TRAHERNE

HEAVEN

We might have confused ideas about what or where heaven is, but we can see it as a part of the love that goes on and on, even after death. It is being in the presence of God.

God is preparing a heavenly city for you.

HEBREWS 11:16

We are waiting for a new heaven and a new earth in which justice dwells.

2 PETER 3:13

He is able for all time to save those who draw near to God through him, since he always lives to make intercession for them.

HEBREWS 7:25

*I am the good shepherd. The good shepherd lays down
his life for the sheep… My sheep hear my voice, and
I know them, and they follow me; and I give them
eternal life, and they shall never perish, and no one
shall snatch them out of my hand.*

JOHN 10:11, 27–28

*In my Father's house are many rooms; if it were not so,
would I have told you that I go to prepare a place for
you? … I will come again and will take you to myself.*

JOHN 14:2, 3

*God himself will be with them; he will wipe away every
tear from their eyes, and death shall be no more, neither
shall there be mourning nor crying nor pain any more,
for the former things have passed away.*

REVELATION 21:3–4

*In his love he wraps and holds us.
He enfolds us for love and he will never let us go.*

DAME JULIAN OF NORWICH

*The Lord bless you and keep you.
The Lord make his face to shine upon you,
and be gracious to you:
The Lord lift up his countenance upon you,
and give you peace.*

NUMBERS 6:24–26

Our Father who art in heaven,
Hallowed be thy name.
Thy kingdom come,
Thy will be done,
On earth as it is in heaven.
Give us this day our daily bread,
And forgive us our trespasses,
As we forgive those who trespass against us.
And lead us not into temptation,
But deliver us from evil.
For thine is the kingdom, the power and the glory,
For ever and ever. Amen.

THE LORD'S PRAYER